THE RIGHTEOUSNESS OF GOD IN CHRIST

The Righteousness of God in Christ

Jean Jeter

ISBN: 978-1-962363-88-4 Paperback
ISBN: 978-1-962363-89-1 Ebook

Rev. date: 04/03/2024

INTRODUCTION

I was naive to the workings of the world when I was growing up. I believed God was alive and well and everyone loves everyone. You want to be good and spread love as the good book says. You don't see the evil in the hearts of man. You go to church and everyone is praising God and all is right with the world. It is an eye-opener when you find out that Satan is undercover and a wolf in sheep's clothing looking to steal, kill and destroy your faith and take away your spiritual joy and spiritual innocence.

Another eye-opener that I realized is, that as long as you live in a world of ignorance about who the Father is, Satan won't bother you. He likes you living in ignorant s and sleeping in God's almighty power. However, once things in your life goes wrong and you start to question why when you have done all the good things that God instructed you to do that draws attention to satan. He knows when you start to ask questions you are on a spiritual journey and you start looking for answers to your questions. The answer to those questions will lead you into God's righteousness. However, when you really understand the ways of God Satan starts to make you doubt God's love for you. Satan will use your hardship to make you question your beliefs and faith. This is good because you are now awake your spiritual journey begins.

My prayer is that anyone who reads this book will get the ultimate message, which is. God loves you no matter who you are or what you have done. God is a God of Righteousness and in his righteousness forgiveness, mercy and grace will endure forever.

DEDICATION TO MY MOTHER

Minerva Marie Watkins (Brogden)

Mama named me Minerva Jean, my first name after her. My middle name Jean, means, Gift from God and God is gracious. I always used my middle name because Minerva is an old name. The meaning of Minerva is a Roman Goddess of Wisdom, Justice, Law, Victory and the sponsor of Arts, trade and strategy.

A person's name is supposed to be a reflection of who they are. My given name Minerva, is an honor to have. Since I have grown up I have met other ladies, not a lot, with this name and they all wear their name Minerva well.

When you are a child you feel embarrassed, when children make fun of you because your name is different. I was very shy. My name, as wonderful as the meaning is, as a child, it made me stand out when my name was called. I felt like the odd one in the group.

I used my middle name so I could fit in. When I am out if I hear someone calling me Minerva Jean that is a family member or children I grew up with. If I hear someone calling me Jean they are high school friends, people I work with and or church members.

So, I dedicate this book to you mama, who has lived and raised children in a God given Righteous way and is in the arms of our Heavenly Father in Heaven. I thank her for giving me a name that has so much meaning both the first and the middle and for the most part of my life, I have tried to live up to it.

Mom I use my God-given name **MINERVA JEAN** as I dedicate this book to you.

I Love you and miss you with all my heart your loving daughter MINERVA JEAN.

ABOUT MYSELF

I am a child of the King. However, on my journey I have had to learn that just saying and repeating God's word does not show the true meaning without studying the word. Walking the walk in His way shows my true self and who I am in Christ. However, without study, you only have half of the understanding of the word.

As I acknowledge the God in my life and I study His word then I have to verbalize it. I then realized that the meaning goes deeper than just hearing his word but doing His word. All of God's word has more power and has more wisdom in it than we will ever know. God's word is a mystery that we will not know or understand.

We all have a cross to bear and there are no exemptions. We will all deal with trials and tribulations. These will produce in me long-suffering, character, hope and patience. Through all of these hardships, weeping may endure for a night but joy will come in the morning. In between my weeping and joy I have had to learn how to depend on the Father for my strength and faith. My joy will bring joy to the Lord and glorify his holy name. That is my purpose in life to glorify my Lord for the good times and the bad. The bad times will show me who is in control of my life by carrying out his purpose for my life.

So, I ask all of you to not just read the bible but study it. Pray for wisdom, understanding, and discernment. May I also ask that you sit down with your children on your journey. Don't leave them out there with half of the truth. The most important thing to teach them about our Father in heaven is forgiveness and obedience.

God bless and keep you.

MY SPIRITUAL JOURNEY

My Spiritual journey was wrapped up in God as a child. He belongs to me and only me. That was my child's view of God. As I matured I realized just the opposite. People were not all loving and caring but could be downright mean. I had to start my journey by asking questions, why are people not following God's way of living? I know a lot of people say they are living a Christian life. However, they are not following the order that God has lay- ed out for them. You soon learn that good and evil walk hand and hand. You learn that God has given us free will to walk as he does. However, you also realize everyone does not choose the way of the Lord.

The righteousness of God in Christ is about the way we choose to live. We need to walk, talk and live out the word of God. Living in righteousness is not easy. We have too many distractions from God's word. The flesh and the order does not go hand and hand. They contradict each other. It is impossible to live righteous before God on your own. God is the only one who can bring you to righteousness living in this world. The Whole Armor of God is your protection, wisdom, understanding and discernment. Through trial and error, I had to grow to understand and be aware of God's rigorousness. The Whole Armor of God is your expression of your trust in God knowing he will never leave you are forsaken you. We put on our armor by seeking his word above everything else. **THE BELT OF TRUTH:** around your waist so you can stand firm in his word which is the word of God. It is put around the waist to hold believers together for their protection. **THE BREASTPLATE OF RIGHTEOUSNESS:** means to obey God in all you do. This gives Him honor. It is the process of sanctification that helps kill the flesh and defeat the enemy. It also helps to identify UN-righteousness and immoral behavior. **THE SANDALS:** which prepare you to spread the Gospel of Peace. They are fitted for your feet to make you ready to stand firm on your Christian foundation. **THE SHIELD OF FAITH:** A believer's protection in trusting God's power to extinguish all flaming arrows of evil. **THE SWORD OF THE SPIRIT:** which is the word of God, which is what we should live by. It helps us pray in the spirit on all occasions and with all prayer requests. **THE HELMET OF SALVATION:** it is the final act of readiness in your preparation for combat with evil. The helmet is vital for survival, protecting the brain, the command station for the rest of the body. If the head was badly damaged the head of the armor would be of little use. When armor is put on it works together for our salvation. The Helmet of Salvation is your protection for your ears from satans words of war.

The Righteousness of God in Christ opens you up to godly living. Before you can live righteous you have to know what and how righteous living looks like. I hope this book encourages you to live right before God. Live in trust and hope and the expectancy of a life worth living, to glorify being a child of the king.

FORWARD

The Righteousness of Gods in Christ

As I began to write this book my thoughts were about "The Righteousness of God in Christ". As I wrote I ask myself what is righteous? You know we use a lot of words in the bible. We use words in sentences, we use these words to express ourselves, but do we really know what the word means.

Righteousness is one of the chief attributes of God. Chief Attributes means the main concern of ethical behavior. Ethical behavior means being honest, being honorable, showing humanity, to your Christian brothers and sisters in Christ. Be virtuous and have a clean conscience. We will look at some of the ethical behaviors, that will make you righteous before God or unrighteous depending on your behavior. We need to be cautious that we not only talk about our righteousness but also be righteous in the way we treat people.

The qualities of a righteous person are being happy in the Lord, he does not walk in the counsel of the ungodly nor does he stand in the pathway of the sinners, nor does he sit in the seat of the scoffers, his delight is in the law of the lord, and he meditates day and night in God's Law.

As you read my book you will find that sometimes I put just the chapter and not the verses. God wants you to read the bible verses before and after to get the whole meaning of his word. People pick and choose the verse from the bible that meets their needs, not realizing their selfishness to be right. This is also a sin against God. The answers to all of the questions are in the bible if you take your time to read understand and ask God for the wisdom you need to grow in Christ. God's word is a mystery, so if you can find the answer reverse the question. Example: Forgiveness, they hurt me and I can't find it in my heart to forgive. I've done all God has asked me. The reversed question: what was my part in this situation.

It takes at least two to make a situation where forgiveness is needed. Don't be too proud to see your part in it. Maybe you need to apologize.

THE WORD OF GOD FOR
THE PEOPLE OF GOD

EPHESIANS 2:1 -5

And you were dead in your trespasses and sins, in which you previously walked according to the ways of the world, according to the rulers who exercise authority over the lower heavens, the spirit now working in the disobedience. We too also lived among them in our fleshly desires. We carry out the inclinations of our flesh and thoughts, and we were by nature children under wrath as the others were also. But as God is rich in mercy, and because of His great love that He had for us, He made us alive with the Messiah even though we were dead in our trespasses. You are saved by grace.

As the Father meets us at our needs we are all at different levels of growth. He may be trying to turn us from a situation that will lead us to destruction. You may be in a situation where God is testing your trust and faith in him. The place where you are may be the place you are supposed to be. God uses all situations to help us grow in our spiritual walk with him. You might have traveled this road before, and you were hard-headed you tired to solve your own problems instead of reaching out to God. You go on make the wrong decision because you are in your own wisdom instead of depending on the Father. We have a way of thinking we have all the answers to all of our problems. Because we don't reach out to God and listen to that small voice, that might say stop, not now, be patient we ignore it because we know what we want and we want it now. This is the test from God; are you relying on yourself or do you depend on your faith, that God will see you through.

If you find yourself in a situation that is or has caused you heartache or pain you might know of someone who is going through the same situation. You can tell them how your faith and His mercy has brought you through. Even if you recognize that the situation is somewhat the same remember we are all different people, we think differently and we deal with things differently. The Father's test is for each individual depending on their walk with God, make sure you are not getting in His way trying to be helpful to someone else. We all have our own individual trials and tribulations to deal with.

The best instruction is to tell them to go to God in Prayer. Tell them to steal away to God for direction and to enlighten them as to what he is trying to work out in their lives. Explain to them that God speaks to everyone who has an ear to listen. Praying for a clean heart and an upright spirit will give them a clear vision. Do not pray about the problem pray for wisdom and discernment into the problem. We should all seek first the kingdom of heaven and everything else will be added to them according to his riches in glory.

After you have directed them to God then take your hands off. Once you have prayed for them and told them about God's goodness, his grace and mercy it is then up to them to choose who they will follow, God or the world.

WHEN GOD SPEAKS ABOUT RIGHTIOUSNESS

God speaks through thoughts and feelings of the Holy Spirit. When He speaks he brings feelings of peace and his voice resonates. A voice that we recognize because He knows us and we his sheep hear his voice. He meets us where we are and his voice fills our hearts.

When God speaks he does not chatter as in gossip. When God speaks, he does not speak to hear himself talk but always with a purpose. His purpose in speaking is always to lead, guide and direct his children on their pathway to righteousness. However, God does not speak just to his children but to everyone who has ears to hear, let them listen and hear what saith the Lord.

One of God's purposes is to get your attention to obey and learn. Whether you listen and obey, or try to obey and fail, it doesn't matter. As long as you seek God first in everything you do always listen to that small voice. If you decide you don't want to obey what you hear, or you don't believe what you hear, that is your choice. However, when God's word goes out it doesn't not return to him void.

In my spiritual journey I have always been blessed, not with the blessings of the world but with love for my brothers and sisters in Christ. I have been blessed with the endurance to fight the battle ahead, the strength to pick myself up after I fall down and faith that no matter what befalls me I am not alone. I have also been blessed with the craving desire to know my Father in all parts of my life.

As we have learned to listen to God's voice we sometimes become confused about the Christian life. Sometimes the world can drown out his voice. That is when doubts, confusion and our faith is shaken. God is our Father of love, respect, compassion, everything that is good. However, the world we live in is anything but righteous. I know we live in a fallen world and that is the thing we have to be reminded of. When we realize the heartbreak, pain and the evil things that are thrust upon us and the things we do to each other they are from the evil of this fallen world. Always keep your eyes on the prize in Christ Jesus.

TRUE RIGHTEOUSNESS OF GOD

ROMANS 1: 16

For I am not ashamed of the gospel, because it is the power of God that brings salvation to everyone who believes: first to the Jew, then to the Gentile. For in the gospel the righteousness of God is revealed- a righteousness that is by faith from first to last, just as it is written. The righteous will live by faith.

ROMANS

The righteousness of God comes through faith in Jesus Christ. Mere belief in God is insufficient. This must come first but faith in Jesus is required for salvation.

ROMANS 3: 11

There is no one righteous, not even one. No one understands; none seeks God. All have trued away all alike have become useless. There is not one who does what is good, not even one. Their throat is an open grave; they deceive with their tongues. Vipers venom is under their lips. Their mouth is full of cursing and bitterness. Their feet are swift to shed blood; ruin and wretchedness are in their paths, and the path of peace they have not known. There is no fear of God before their eyes.

ROMANS 3 :20 23

For no one will be justified in His sight by the works of the law because the knowledge of sin comes through the law.

For all have sinned and fallen short of the glory of God. They are justified freely by His grace through the redemption that is in Christ Jesus.

PROVERBS 18 :10

The name of Yahweh is a strong tower; the righteous run into and they are protected.

PSALM 1 1:–3

How happy is the man who does not follow the advice of the wicked or take the path of sinners or join a group of mockers! Instead, his delight is in the Lord's instruction, and he meditates on it day and night. He is like a tree planted beside streams of water that bears its fruit in season and whose leaf does not wither. Whatever he does prospers.

GOD RIGHTEOUS ORDER

FIRST CORINTHIAN: CHAPTER 14 VERSE 40

Order is done in a neat, logical and organized way. Order is putting the right people in the right order based on the gifts God has instilled upon us. God's universe is orderly. He created everything in orderly sequences and he did it in a six-day span. And on the seventh day he rested and it was complete. This sequence of order set the world in motion and God's righteousness was no exception. Our bodies are an example of God's orderliness. The heart pumps blood through organs, the brain is the control center and it sends thousands of messages per second to regulate pain, temperature, respiration, brain patterns and thoughts to our bodies.

This is why God's acts of righteousness are so important. Your acts of righteousness put you in order for God's blessings. Do you remember the little song that children use to sing; boys and girls sitting in a tree, kissing, first comes love then comes marriage then comes a baby in a baby carriage.

That is the order that God put into place. This order was to keep families together, make strong family connections and stop unwanted babies. These babies are meant to be a gift from God and not a hindrance. God's order stops diseases and God's order for righteousness keeps you in line for his greatest blessings.

GENESES: Paraphrased, In the beginning. God created the heaven and the earth. The earth was formless, empty, darkness covered the surface of the watery depths and the Spirit of God was hovering over the surface of the water. This is God's order for our existence.

THE FIRST DAY: God said "Let there be light and there was light. He separated the light from the darkness. God called the light day and the darkness night. He called it day and night. Evening came and the morning; the first. **And God saw that it was good.**

THE SECOND DAY: God said "Let there be an expanse separating the water from the water and God separated the water under the expanse from the water above and called it the sky. **And God saw it was good.**

THE THIRD DAY: Then God said "Let the water under the sky be gathered into one place, and the dry land appear. And it was so. God called the dry land earth and Called the gathering of the water seas. **And God saw that it was good.** God said let the earth produce vegetation seed-bearing plants and fruit tree on the earth and bearing fruit with seeds in it according to their kind. And it was so. **And God saw that it was good.**

THE FOURTH DAY: God said "Let there be light in the expanse of the sky to separate day and night. The expanse of the sky provides light for the earth. God made two great lights, the greater light to have dominion overt the day and the lesser light to have dominion over the night as well as the stars, **God saw that it was good.**

THE FIFTH DAY: God said: Let the water swarm with living creatures, birds fly above the earth. God created sea creatures, so every living creature that moves and swarms in the water according to their kind also winged birds according to their kind. God blessed them. Then He said to them "be fruitful, fill the waters and the seas and let the birds multiply on earth. **And God saw it was good.**

THE SIXTH DAY: Then God said, "Let **US** make man in **OUR** image according to our likeness. they will rule the fish of the sea and the birds of the sky, the lives stock all of the earth and the creatures that crawl on the earth. God blessed them and God said to them; be fruitful, multiply, fill the earth and subdue it. **GOD SAW THAT ALL HE HAD MADE WAS VERY GOOD.**

THE SEVENTH DAY: So, the heavens and the earth and everything in them were completed. By the seventh day God had completed His work that he has done and He rested on the seventh day from all His work. God Blessed the Seventh day and declared it Holy, for on it He rested from His work of the creation. I paraphrased Geneses the Creation, to allow you the image of God's Order. God does not half-step. He is meticulous in his order. Everything is in order from the beginning of time. God made us in his image out of love for us. Anything less than the Father's orders is no order at all and is disrespectful to God.

The creation is without doubt both amazing and awesome without question. The creation reveals God's character and nature. This reveals to us that we are not the makers of our own fate but the makers of our universe and our lives hopes and dreams. We are the stewards of his creation. The way we reverend His world and the respect we give to each other shows our appreciation of his love for us.

God has an order for the family. God has to be first in your family. That means that we teach our children about the love of God and that we are all his children. We even as adults need to realize that God is the head of our home and no matter how old we are we are still his children.

God's order for the spouse. The husband is the head of the house whole next to God. The spouse takes his direction from God and passes it on to his wife. Together they show the power of God's love, protection, and they show the blessing that will rain down on them when they are on one accord with God. How much do we miss when we corrupt God's order based on who we think we are compared to who the Father of the universe is.

God's order for children. Children need to understand that they have a father on earth but the Father of all fathers is in Heaven. The working order for the family is God, first and then the daddy, mama and child. Children need to understand that together the mother and the earthly father work together with God to provide for them. the parent's job is to produce godly children that turn into godly adults under the orders of God.

There is also Divine Chaos, this is when the intelligence and the flow of consciousness of God's energy is ignored. When this happens, our life is so disrupted that you in up not knowing what the right hand or the left hand is doing. If your family is not right with God's order your family is broken. This is when the Divine order is broken because you have gone against the rules and laws of God.

Psalm 37: 23-24 A man's steps are established by the Lord and He takes pleasure in his ways. Though he falls, he will not be overwhelmed, because the Lord holds our hands.

We all lose our way when it comes to order. Went things go backwards, remember God knew you were trying to do your best. Maybe your going backwards is Gods way of waking you up that he is still there or you could be on the right track but God is sending you on a detour to impart more wisdom into your journey.

Don't fret God does not leave his children and don't leave God, be patient and listen to his small voice. Our bodies are the example of God's order. The heart pumps blood through organs, the brain sends thousands of messages per second to regulated, pain, temperature, perspiration, and thoughts.

This is why God's acts of righteousness are so important. Our acts of righteous put us in order for God's blessing. Do you remember the little jingle the children use to sing, Boy and girl sitting in a tree, k i s s i n g. first comes love then come marriage then come baby in a baby carriage. That is the order that God put into place. This order was to keep families together, make strong family connections, stop unwanted babies which are a gift from God and not a hindrance. God's order stops diseases and God's order for righteousness keeps us in line for his greatness blessing.

GOD'S RIGHTEOUS LOVE

First Corinthian 13 v 4 God does not leave anything to chance. Love is patient, Love is Kind, Love does not envy, is not boastful, is not conceited, does not act improperly, is not selfish, is not provoked and does not keep a record of wrongs. Love finds no joy in unrighteousness but rejoices in the truth. It bears all things, believes all Things hopes all things, endures all things, Love never ends.

Before you say you love someone make sure it is love and not lust. These are the Guidelines. Christian women's definition of love is much different than that of a non-believer A non-believer throws out all the rules and goes for what he knows. A believer even though they break the rules also, they learn from their mistakes through disobedience of the stumbling block which is Jesus.

There are different types of love that we should know. These types of love you will understanding of the types of love you will encounter. This is another guide to be aware of.

Storage: Empathy Bond/ Familiar love: Empathy is the ability to understand and share the feeling of another. **Philos: is a Friend Bond.** It is not to be found in any other relationship. It is unique in that it links two people who look out for each other. **Eros is Romantic love:** It is an emotional feeling with strong attraction toward another person. It is the situation within intimate relationships. **Agape Love: It is Unconditional Love.** This is God's Love for us. It is selfless, and sacrificial. It is the highest of all love. Giving of charity out of the goodness of your heart. It is doing for others whether you know them or not, just because they are in need. **Ludus Love: This is playful Love.** This is childlike flirtation love. This happens usually in the beginning of a relationship. This consists of teasing, playful motives, laughter between two people. Pragma **Love: This is Enduring Love.** It is everlasting love between a couple that chooses to put equal effort into their relationship. Commitment and dedication are required for each. Instead of falling in love you are standing in love with the partner you want to be by your side indefinitely.

These are just a few of the loves we experience in our relationships. All of these describe God's love for us. The Father is a God of **Storge Love** and is very **emphatic** of our feelings. He understands what we are going through. At this time when he shows us love and understanding and he empathizes with what we are going through. This is when he takes the time that he draws close to you.

Then there is a time when he is your **Philo Friend**. He holds you in his hands and lets you know that this to will pass. He lets know he is your friend who is closer than a brother and he will never leave your side. Having a friend when you feel you are all alone, God's word gives you peace.

God is the **God of Ergo Love,** this is romantic and intimate love. He is your first love the lover of your soul. This is when you have taken time to get to know him in all his ways. God needs your love as much as he wants you to love him. He wants you to depend on him for all of your needs. When you are in a romantic love, you want that person to take time out for you, so does the Father. Then there is **Agape Love.** This is the most love you can give a person **Unconditional Love:** this is the only love that is complete.

No matter what you do, no matter how bad, disgusting, unfeeling, unforgivable, you feel you are God will always love you. All he sees is love. God knows where we came from, he knows what is in our hearts and just like parents are supposed to be he never stops loving his children. **Ludus Love, is playful Love.** Has God ever made you laugh at yourself. Have you ever seen something funny and said God must have a sense of humor while you are laughing. Have you ever read the bible and said no he didn't and laughing. God has a sense of humor. He has to because we have a sense of humor and we are made in his image. Then there is **Prama which is Enduring Love,** which is when you and the Father go through all kinds of changes in your relationship. You have doubts about your faith, about God's promises to you, your feeling of whether he is with you like he said when you are down and out. There are times when you are in tears and don't know which way to go. This is the time when you say I'm giving up, and then you fall back on the words, if God said it I believe it and it will be done. You then realize that God is loving you every step of the way. God knows that God wants you to put what you believe into practice. This is a standoff because you are determined not to let go of his unchanging hands and he in his unchanging love ill not let you go. You are standing in Love with the Father.

GOD OF PEACE

SECOND CORINTHIAN 13:11 finally, brothers, rejoice. Become mature, be encouraged, be of the same mind, be at peace, and the god of love and peace will be with you. Greet each other with a holy kiss. All the saints greet you.

God's peace is not in your surroundings but on the inside where God dwells. Peace is something very few of us understand. The only way to experience true peace is through prayer and accept where you are after prayer and supplication and let God lead the way. At this time you need to accept what God wants for you, even though you don't see it, which means he is putting everything in order in the background. This will be one of the hardest things to do in the name of patience and faith. This is a part of your spiritual journey.

Sometimes when we pray we think this is a done deal. We think that what we pray for will jump out of the sky and into our lap. When we pray for people and situations we think it will just come to pass right away. This is where you lose your peace. Our faith is tested and sometimes we can feel hopeless. The truth is our god is a God of order. In this order he has to put everything in His place. Sometimes that takes God's timing because God is not just interested in your request but in the spiritual life and growth of all involved.

We have to realize that God is depending on us to depend on Him through faith. Accepting where you are and knowing that god will sustain you in all of your endeavors with give you the peace you need to move forward. Peace comes when you understand that He is in control and working to bring you to where he wants you to bed.

Life is like a roller coaster ride. Everything that goes wrong we blame on God. STOP... when do we start asking ourselves what am I missing? I know what we as not has humans are missing. We took our life out of God's hands and gave our peace away. I know because I have done it. While I was trying to get a loan I could not afford, in my head I had figured out how I could handle it. It's called rob Peter to pay Paul. Then I read this poem.

SO, PLANT YOUR OWN GARDEN AND DECORATE YOUR OWN SOUL, INSTEAD OF WAITING FOR SOMEONE TO BRING YOU FLOWERS.... And you learn, you really can endure, that you really are strong and you really do have self worth.

I kept reading it before I signed the paper to the loan. That was not my only mistakes I have made without understanding that God is talking to us, through his word, friends and circumstances. We need to be aware of his voice. After I read it over and over I knew God was trying to tell me something. It was too late. My need for doing it my instead of God's way and leading me into frustration and again wondering how am I going to get through this.

The poem was saying to me to get my own life together in Christ. Let him beautify my life with his garden of faith and love. Stop waiting for the world to solve my problems and let Christ bring me flowers of peace to my life that will never die.

We always have our hands out to the world to resolve the problems we make for ourselves. It is not until we have gone around and around and find ourselves in the same situation we realize there has got to be a better way and that way is Christ. We understand the we don't know everything and we don't have our life under control.

This has been one of the hardest lessons I have had to learn on my Christian journey. However I have never lost my faith, it has been shaken and tears have run down my face. I have ask questions of which there was no answer. However, after it was said and done and I am on my knees, I fine peace that it will be alright. I was going to say I never lost my praise but that would not be true. We all go through times that in our own belief we can not find peace.

Understand that God's word applies to everyone, but everyone does not apply His principles to their lives. Gods words are a mystery we shall not all see , hear or understand. This is when we should always pray for wisdom, understanding and discernment. This is where we find peace as we accept God's word, love, faith, grace and mercy through his Agape love.

GOD OF SPIRITUAL WISDOM

1ST CORINTHIAN CHAPTER 2 However, we do speak a wisdom among the mature, but not a wisdom of this age, or of the rulers of this age, who are coming to nothing. On the contrary, we speak God's hidden wisdom in a mystery, a wisdom God predestined before the ages of our glory. None of the rules of this age knew this wisdom, for if they had known it, whey would not have crucified the Lord of glory. But the unbeliever does not welcome what comes from God's Spirit, because it is foolishness to him; he is not able to understand it since it is evaluated spiritually The spiritual person, however, can evaluate everything, yet he himself cannot be evaluated by anyone. But we have the mind of Christ.

Sometimes when God gives us wisdom about something, we think that no one else is as wise as we are. Your wisdom is only one side of the coin. You are not the only one God gives wisdom to. If you listen when wisdom is spoken, take time to ask God for understanding and discernment. This is why we should keep out mouth close and our hears open. If you do that you will add more wisdom and understanding to what you think you know. Listening to wisdom will give you another view of the information God has already given you.

Have you ever wondered why the unbelievers don't see the wrong of the world. They do not live humble before the Lord. They think that human wisdom in their own self is the answer. They will even go so far as to quote scripture and turning the word around to make their actions acceptable. They can kill and hate and demand their rights and feel no remorse. They will find a verse in the bible to justify their evil and unacceptable actions. That is another reason we need to study the bible to know when you are dealing with evil.

We as Christian have been given spiritual wisdom, knowledge and understanding of the wisdom of the word. If we lack wisdom all we have to do is ask and it will be given to us. God has imparted in us hidden wisdom. for it say in 1ˢᵗ Corinthians Chapter 2 Verse 9 Eye hath not seen, nor ear heard, Neither have entered into the heart of man, The things which God hath prepared for them that love him

GOD OF WISDOM -True wisdom consists primarily of two parts: the knowledge of God, and the knowledge of ourselves. If you lack knowledge, go to school, If you lack wisdom, get on you knees! Knowledge is not wisdom. Wisdom is the proper use of knowledge.

GOD OF HUMILITY

PHILIPPIANS 2:3 Christians Humility

Do nothing out of rivalry or conceit, but in humility consider others as more important than yourselves. Everyone should look out not only for his own interest, but also for the interest of others.

The purpose of humility is that none of you will be inflated with pride and favor of one person over the another. What makes you feel you are better than anyone else, without love of God we would all cease to exist. Humility makes you humble before your accusers. To walk in humility you can not boast of anything because it is not through your effort that you obtain what you have. God is the one who gives you Grace, Mercy, Wisdom, Understand and Discernment to move ahead. It is only through your prayer life that God allows you to succeed.

Being to proud about what you think you know instead of being humble in the situation puts humility on the back burner. you have used your own wisdom instead of humility to deal with the person you are in opposition to. Try to be honorable in everyone eyes. Humility means, sometimes you have to walk away, it does not mean proving your point so you will look like the winner and the other the loser. This leaves the impression you are aggressive and unapproachable.

A person who walks in humility will cause people with an evil heart to back away from the spirit within. You will cause them to see who they really are. Humility is a forgiving spirit that gives you compassion and empathy for the person who has wronged you. This is hard for a person who's life has been turned around and the only thing they have left is bitterness. When you walk in humility you walk in Gods love and it shows. There will people who will not understand how you can be so humble when people are stepping all over you, just say it is a gift from God and walk proudly in it. God sees the way you walk in your humility and you will be rewarded.

Being humble means seeing the other side of the coin before you react. You will find yourself asking is this worth the argument, is it that important. I was once approached by a woman in church. I came in getting ready to enjoy the service. Before I knew it she was up in my face accusing me of something I knew nothing about. Soon people were coming in and a small crowd was gathering. When I could get a word in edge wise I said, let's go into the other room to talk, I knew to whom she was referring. When we closed the door, I explained the confusion and she calmed down. Had I responded in the way she approached me, we both would be out of order and embarrassed. This lady was usually very nice so I knew that she was really at the end of her patience. She apologized and told me how sorry she was. Had I respond like she approached me it could have really been bad, for nothing.

GOD OF MORALITY

MORALITY: Another word for morality is ethics which are standards that enable people to live cooperatively in groups and understandings of what is right or wrong. Some of the things that morals are associated with is, telling the truth, keeping promises, not judging and many more. All of these can destroy lives when morals are disrespected. However, of all of the morals, sexual immorality, once you disrespect a persons heart, and body it can not be undone. It effects the future of others and how they move on in their lives. sex is used as a weapons to use and abuse. Sex is emotional and controls your mind as to what you think about yourself.

SEX is not recreational, to be used as a substitute for proving how much of a man or women you are to get your sexual needs met.

First Corinthian Chapter 5:

It is widely reported that there is sexual immorality among you, the type that is not even tolerated among the gentiles. A man is living with his father's wife and inflated with pride instead of being filled with grief so that he who has committed this act might be removed from your congregation. I am absent in the body but present in spirit, I have already decided about the one who has done this thing as though I were present.

Does this sound familiar. This book of the bible was written centuries ago and we still are dealing with sexual immorality. Since the sexual revolution of this age all forms of sex is accepted outside of marriage. Friends with Benefits has added to the saying why buy the milk when can get the cow with no benefit of commitment.

Men and women who are trying to follow Christian doctrine find it hard to find a mate. Looking for a serious relationship, a one on one relationship respecting and loving the one you are with. Finding a relationship that is inclusive is hard. Satan hates happiness in Christians or anyone else. In this age there is nothing sacred about sex. It is more visible then ever and it is accepted. Our children see it at home, on TV and hear it in the music they listen to. Our children pattern themselves after entertainers who wear clothes either to short or too low without shame. Sex trafficking is at an all time high.

Morals have gone out the window. Our children and adults are following the ways of the world and the adults are leading the way. There are babies born out of wedlock or should I say, out of unstable relationships between a man and a women. Usually it is unstable due to sexual immorality which leads to sex additions.

The word wedlock is foreign to the sexual community. The reason I use community because there are women and young girls who are having babies by two or three different men. The women blame the men the men blame the women. It is both of their faults. If you want to use sex as a play tool at least be respectful of your bodies.

Babies are born with low birth rate, infant morality, born into poverty and low income families, not to mention crack babies.. Ladies need to realize that the baby you bring into this world, if you are out there just having fun, is your baby. Your body carried that child. Your body went through the hardship of label, why be with a man who does not appreciate what we as women go through. If the man does not step up no matter what the law says it is on you.

These babies who are unloved, unwanted, UN cared for are a problem to society. Any child brought into this world deserves the best that a man and women has to offer. If you cant give them that then think twice before you lay down just for fun for it because you like the way the opposite sex look. Sex is not a game.

I heard one man laugh at the Christian women because she wanted a christian man. His response "I guess they are waiting for Jesus to come back, as he laughed it off". A christian man in marriage means, love, companionship, respect, stability, comfort, wholeness, love, protection, but most of all a Christian partner in Christ. A Christian relationship in Christ holds a marriage together. God is the center of all relationships. This is why we have to be equally yoked. Marriage to the right person, is like a cake and sex is the icing that pulls it all together. It is the best part of both of them.

ROMANS C1 VS 24 – 26

Therefore God gave them over in the sinful desires of hearts sexual impurity for degrading of their body one with another. They exchanged the truth about God for a lie, and worshiped and served created things rather than the Creator – who is forever praised. Amen.

Because of this God gave them over to shameful lusts. Even their women exchanged natural sexual relations for unnatural ones. In the same way the men also abandoned natural relations with women and were inflamed with lust for one another. Men committed shameful acts with other, men and received in themselves the due penalty for their error.

Furthermore, just as they did not think it worthwhile to retain the knowledge of God, so God gave then over to a depraved mind, so that they do what ought not to be done.

As I was writing about righteous Judgment, I realize that judgment is one the most profound righteousness the world has to acknowledge. Judgment takes a tole on the character of the world. Look around and see what is happening in the world. All of the hate, destruction, lost souls who are suffering, immortality, disrespect for the word of God.

Are we judging by our standards or Gods principals? When we judge are we reflecting Gods grace and mercy? Are we judging righteously. Are we thinking that we are the epitome of truth and we sit as judgment of others based on our principals rather than Gods? The wronful judgment can destroy a persons life. There are some sins that can destroy the word of God and his kingdom. The judgment of these sins can condemn before all information is presented. Remember that God will not be mocked.

When we judge righteously remember that God is the judge of all. While you are judging someones sin, God is judging you. If the sin is against his kingdom, and the sin defiled the word of God, shake the dust off your feet separating them from you and their actions from God. God is the only true judge. While we are judging, lets ask ourselves, in our judgment or we judging bye our beliefs in God or man's? Are we playing judge and jury?

JOEL 3:16

The Lord ROARING LIKE A LION from Jerusalem; his loud voice will thunder from that city, and the sky and the earth will shake.

1 PETER 5:8-10

Be self-controlled and alert. Your enemy the devil prowls around LIKE A ROARING LION looking for someone to devour, but God is our hiding place, we run into the shelter of his wings and we are saved. Resist him, standing firm in the faith, because you know in that your brothers throughout the world are undergoing the same kind of suffering.

As you can see the devil is a deceiver. He mocks God with Gods own words. We are the ones he is trying to devour. We all need to pray for discernment, wisdom, understanding. We need to pray that we judge, with Gods principal and not the deceiver.

JAMES 1:19-20

Let every person be quick to hear, slow to speak slow to anger; for the anger of man does not produce the righteousness of God.

I see people jumping on the band wagon of judgment daily. Even though you might be right what is your motivation. God is revealing to the world the deceivers, sometimes we need to step back and let God do his work. Judgement should come in the form of grace. Without graceful judgement they will continue on their same path. Judging a Person or not judging a person can be just as harmful. We judge people on what we see instead of who they really are.

MATTHEW 7 VS 15

States, Beware of false prophets, who come to you in sheep's clothing, but underneath are ravenous wolves.

What are the reasons for judging others, is it because we have such high regards for a person and what they seems to represent? When they fall we are the first to judge, because we feel like a fool for trusting them. Could it be because some of you are jealous of their fame and fortune? Could it be because you want the fame and adoration they are receiving? Do you judge because you don't believe in God, so you can say I told you God is a fake and He doesn't exist.

We all judge differently based on how we feel about that persons personae, how we feel about ourselves, the earthy wealth and accolade (Mark of acknowledgment and receives the highest praise) and where we are in our own spiritual walk. Righteous judgment need to put in its rightful place, and order and with grace and mercy. Your judgment is nothing compared to the judgment that men will endure when they betray God.

Let's look at another form of judgment. Judgment that effects the fabric of godly livings. The judgment that I spoke of before can change the worlds view of God and his righteousness. What about the judgment we do to each other.

Our Children look to us for love guidance, hopes dreams and respect. Out of our mouths comes the words from our own of self hatred that we pass on to our children. We as children of God all want the best for our children. We should rise above any negative thoughts that we think of ourselves and encourage our children with words of strength, and possibilities. The negative words out of our mouths can beat down all the hopes that our children dream of. We have a responsibility to instill in our children, Gods love and his respect for human kind. We, not only as parents but as children of God have to take responsibilities for our children and our fellowman. When love and understanding is needed but not given, we too will be judged.

People who have been cut down by the opinions and judgment of others not to mention the low self-esteem are marked by the judgment of others. These judgments of others come from what they see but not from what they know.

The other side, that you will also be judged by is encouraging your children to feel superior to others. If you cause your children to walk around in pride, which is an excessive love of ones own excellence, you are teaching your children self-centered. A self-centered person, child or adult is of no use to God. This person is so wrapped up in his/her self they can not show the love and companion needed to work in God's Kingdom. We as adults are responsible for our children's spiritual grown and we will be righteously judge accordingly.

MATTHEW 18:6

But whoever cause one of these little ones who believe in Me to stumble, it is better for them to have a large millstone hung around their neck and to be drowned in the depths of the sea.

Judgment without righteousness, judgment out of jealousy, and anger, judgment without compassion, grace and mercy is a destroyer of God's righteousness.

Righteous Judgment is based on all of God's principles, which include the fruits of the spirit, which is charity, joy, peace, patience and kindness, goodness, generosity, gentleness, faithfulness, modesty, self-control chastity. If we judge others without God's grace and mercy we are no better then them. We should take the time to look beyond what we see and realize we all have short comings. We all become what we have experience in our lives. Those experiences good, bad or indifferent mold our life. In our experience lies the reason for our actions.

So if you find that you have a problem judging a persons actions then 'don't. Don't condemn, let God be God. He is a just God, so you should remember; that person is also a child of the King and as God's child he will receive the appropriate judgment.. This is why we should not judge because only God knows the whole story from birth to the present.

When I write I write according to the word of God as He would have us to live. However, I know and you know none of us are perfect. We all fall short of the glory of the most high. We are all guilty of judging.

When we see something that to our understanding is wrong we jump to a judgmental conclusion. However, if you are walking in righteousness as soon as you pass judgment on someone there should be a little voice ,that says who am I to judge? do I know the whole story? Do we pray for the person and the situation they fine themselves in?

We all have been in a position of being judged. Sometimes we end up in situations that we don't know how we got there or how to get out of it.. Maybe it was something that was said in anger and out of place, and judgment takes over. You are now labored, as a liar, cheat, thief etc, and maybe you are. Don t we have a right to go to God in prayer to ask for forgiveness? Don t we have a right to change our ways?

I have found out that Christians will judge you the hardest. They judge you on hear say and what they think they see and know. That is is UN-righteous judgment.

If you are trying to live as christian don't look and wait for a christian to act out of order in their Christian walk. If you look long enough and hard enough you will witness people being human. So lets stop judging them by saying, Uh "she is suppose to be a christian, Christians don't act like that". If you are a christian who are you to judge other Christians.

Let God judge and you and you will not fall under His judgment. These people need to understand we are all prone to mistakes and we are all sinners saved by grace. When you judge and you leave out God's grace and mercy you need to repent ask for forgiveness and revisit Gods word. People don't realize the judgment you give will be the judgment you get.

Your judgment of others might be your test from God. We have to watch unwarranted accusations, because we will be called to the test.

In my writings God always keeps me humble, when I am trying to encourage someone. Before I get through with my thoughts, I know God is going to put me through the test of, patience, trusting and encouragement. He does it all the time. I just wait for it or I'm already in a situation where I haven't been patient and trusting. God is a firm believer in Practice What You Preach. When you are are judging other with UN-righteous judgment God is watching and you are under God judgment as well.

We need to realize that Satan is ready for you to step out of your christian walk. Then he steps in. Satan is there to take your hand and whisper in your ear that the judgment you have just given is correct with out hesitation with on grace or mercy.

JAMES 1;2-4 SAYS

My brothers and sisters, whenever you face trial of any kind, consider it nothing but joy. Because you know that the testing of your faith produces endurance and let endurance have its full effect, so that you may be mature and complete, lacking in nothing and grows in wisdom.

That is why we all need to be quick to listen slow to speak, and slow anger. This gives righteous judgment time to assess the situation before you commit to UN righteous judgment.

We also need to understand that judgment starts with a thought and is followed by the words you speak which turns into actions.

RIGHTEOUS TRUST

JEREMIAH 29:11

For surely I know the plans I have for you, Says the Lord. They are plans for good and not for disaster, to give you a future and a hope. In those days when you pray, I will listen. If you look for me earnest, you will find me when you seek me. I will be found by you, says the Lord.

This is a promise from God. To receive this promise you have to trust the Father and believe that He will do what He says He will do. If you don't trust the Lord in his righteousness that is when you go astray and do it your way.

PROVERBS 3: 5-7
Trust in the Lord with all your heart, do not rely on your own insight. In all your ways acknowledge Him, and he will direct your pathway. Do not be wise in your own eyes, fear the Lord, and turn away from evil. It will be healing for your flesh and refreshment for your body.

I know we have all gotten off of the path God has set for us. We have set down and drawn our plans, decided how we were going to make it work. Then piece by piece the plan it started to fall apart. Most of the plans we want is for money, big house and cars. Some of our dreams are what we see on TV with the rich and famous. We don't realize that what they did to get there , they have to continue to stay there. If our plans are not godly and they do not benefit God Kingdom, it will not last.

We have not ask if this is the plan God has for our life. In our haste we forget that we have a father waiting for us to come to him trusting and realizing that his plan for our life is better than our plans will ever be. You have to have a mind of Christ for your desires to be what God wants for you. If you have a mind for Christ you will only want what he wants for you. He will give you the desires of your heart which will be added to you as you have trusted in him to do his will. Which will glorify his holly name. Your plans should include the gift that God has imparted in you. We all have gifts that will glorify God's name.

PSALMS 27:14
Wait on the Lord; Be strong and let your heart take courage; wait for the Lord.

You get tired of waiting and you think you know better than God. He will then turn you over to your own wisdom. At this time you will feel separated from the Father and you will feel abandoned. You will thirst for His love and His word. It is at this time when you have done all you can do in your way and ignored that small voice in your head; you will then fall to your knees in repentance and ask for forgiveness. Then the Father will open His arm with love and embrace you back unto Himself.

To be righteous in Gods eye you must trust without a doubt that no matter what is happening in your life, you have to trust that God knows from the beginning to the end of your life. He has ordered your steps in His word. Trust in the Lord and stand firm in faith that God will lead, guide and direct you by the Holy Spirit in the way that you should go.

Riches and wealth seduces the mind of man. This is when we try to do it our own way. We need to realize that real wealth is in our love and trust for God and know that He will provide. Seek you first the kingdom of God and his righteousness; and all these things should be added to you.

JOHN 14 VS:27
My peace I leave with you; my peace I give to you. I do not give to you as the world gives. Do no let your hearts be troubled, and do not let them be afraid.

When you find trust in God you find peace. The peace that surpasses all understanding. No matter what circumstances you are in, no matter how hopeless it looks you can walk through it, trusting that God will work things out according to his will for your life.

ISAIAH 43 VS 2
When you pass through the waters, I will be with you; And through the rivers, they shall not overflow you. When you walk through the fire, you shall not be burned Nor shall the flames scorch you. Then God will give you beauty for ashes.

ISAIAH 61 vs 3
And provide for those who grieve in Zion – to bestow on them a crown of beauty instead of ashes, oil of gladness instead of mourning and a garment of praise instead of despair. They will be called the oaks of righteousness, a planting of the Lord for the display of his splendor.

Before you can get Beauty for Ashes, this is the time for brokenness. When you don't trust that God will do what he says he will do. When you don't believe Gods word when He said, what ever you ask in my name I will do so the Father may be glorified; then brokenness has to take place.

ROMANS 9 :

You will be broken as the potter has said, he was shaping for the clay was marred in his hand; so the potter formed it into another pot, shaping it as seemed best to him. God is the potter we are the clay. Brokenness is remolding us into the vessel he can use to glorify his name.

When we are in brokenness God is remolding us daily. He is molding our thought, our actions, the way we deal with people. Every time we fall short of Gods design for us he breaks us and then remolds us to conform to his likeness. Brokenness can be hard, because we are still dealing with the flesh. We are being refined by fire as we go through life. God is purifying our hearts.

Sometimes we are so stuck in the flesh and it is not until we have been broken so many times that we ask God why. Then He is able to open our eyes. Then we receive the message that God has something for us to do and he can't use us the way we are. When we understand this, our lives will change as God begins to use us for his purpose. This is when we have to trust that God knows best. This is the time when we learn not to trust in ourselves but to lean on the Father.

Trusting in God is hard because of the flesh. We want what we want when we want it and we want it now. Trusting and believing go hand and hand. God's timing and our timing is on a different scale. While waiting for Gods direction stay in the word. This is the time to renew your mind. This is the time to learn of Gods principles and how to apply them to your life.

In my experience, trusting in God is the hardest when you see no evident of what you are praying for. This is the time when you get in the most trouble. You follow your own direction.

Patience is a virtue, and without it you loose God best for your life. Being in-patient is a road to nowhere because you go before God and you miss His plan for your life.

GOD'S RIGHTEOUS FORGIVENESS

MATTHEW CHAPTER 6 VERSE 14-15

For if you forgive people their wrong doings, your heavenly father will for give you as well. But if you don't forgive people, your Father will not forgive your wrong doings.

Ephesians 4:32

Be kind to one another, as God in Christ forgave you. Speak and act as those who are going to be judged by the law that gives freedom. For judgment without mercy to the one who has not shown mercy. Mercy triumphs over judgment.

In my spiritual walk I have found that forgiveness is hard. When a friend betrays you there is a layer of pain that goes deep within. That type of hurt goes to the heart of your being. It can happen to male or female friend or to people that or so close they represent your sister, brother mother or father.

In the bible we are to forgive not just 7 times but seven time seventy. There is no numbers of time that we should not forgive if someone ask for forgiveness or when we our self has wronged someone. Just saying you forgive is easy and it is the first step to realizing forgiveness is not just one part. It is not just words it is your feeling to get to peace.

The second step is prayer. Sometimes we want to do as the Lord commands but the pain and anger is hard to deal with. Where we are blessed is knowing God knows our heart. Since he know your true desire is to forgive He will assist you in the process.

We all can unintentionally hurt someones feeling because we are all human. Through these kind of unintentional acts people sometimes can and do hold grudges. Those grudges can do a great deal of harm. Actions can products lies, manipulations and lost of friends. Go to God in prayer. Let God handle your heart as well as the others persons heart. Ask God not only for your forgiveness for hurting someones but ask that they would forgive you. Forgiveness heals deep embedded wounds.

Now lets look at what UN-forgiveness does to the soul. Carrying hurt and anger will make the soul sick. God's wish for all of our lives to be is life of forgiveness. If you are not following Him in forgiveness you will carry around anger, miss judgment of others lack of concentration and it will effect how you deal with other people. All of these can change your personality. Anger makes you strike out at other persons for small things, not to mention you are opening your life up to satans words of hate being spoken in your ears.

PSALMS CHAPTER 19 VERSE 12-14

But who can discern their own errors? Forgive my hidden faults. Keep your servant also from willful sins; may they not rule over me. Then I will be blameless, innocent of great transgression. May these words of my mouth and the mediation of my heart be pleasing in your sight, Lord my Rock and my Redeemer.

PRAYERS TO LIVE BY

IN GOD'S HANDS

Lord your hands are strong and steady and my times are in your hands. Your hands create, guide and direct and they hold and comfort me as no one else can. I know you will protect me in every season of my life and help me face the future with hope.

Thank you Father for having a plan for me because knowing that my life is in your hands give me peace. Your have begun a good work in me in my life and I know you will carry it through to completion until the day of Christ. I am your child thank you for loving and finding value in me when I saw no value in myself.

Lord help me be a women of wisdom and give me the discernment to make right choices that will help me to walk forward as a child of the King. Father sometimes emotions of fear, anger, depression and pride presents their selves to me, please help me to realize that the enemy is busy and he takes every opportunity to cause doubt in my relationship with you.

Please forgive me when I become side tracked and feel as though you know longer love me. Change my heart so that I know that all things work together for the good of those that love the Lord .and are called according to his purpose. Father you know me better than I know myself and you know that no matter what the circumstances and no matter how down I get, you know that you are the only one who can give me peace and rest from my trials and hardships.

Lord thank you for looking at the heart of a person and not the deeds of a person. The deeds that I commit if they are outside of your will then they will not show the Christ in me. Thank you for looking past my false and seeing my needs. Sometimes the needs that are not fulfilled in our time causes us to fall short of the mark. I am asking you to let my light so shine within me that the love may come through.

Help me to trust your ways and empower me to rejoice in hope. I know that what ever happens to me happens for a reason and that reason is to help me to grow in you. It helps to build character, faith, trust and forgiveness. Since I down own myself and I have no control over my life I thank you for holding me in your hands of love and protection.

Amen!!!

PRAYER FOR PATIENCE, STRENGTH AND ENCOURAGEMENT

Phillipians 4:6 do not be anxious about anything, but in everything by prayer and supplication let your requests be made know to God.

Lord give us patience, strength and encouragement to fight the battle that is put before us. Help us to lean and depend on you and not on ourselves. When we are low in spirit give us the mind to call on you and not try to change our situation by ourselves. Help us to move in your spirit and under your direction. We should always remember to praise you in bad times as well as good times because when the praises go up the blessing will come down.

Lord we need you to please watch over us and help us to become what you want us to be. Keep your hands on us so that our territory will be enlarged, because no one can do it better than you. Help us to stand tall and put on the whole armor of God so we can fight off the slings and the arrow of the enemy. Keep reaching out to us and help us be aware of you constant presence. This will be a reminder that we are not alone, so that we will continue to grow in your grace and mercy.

Build a hedge of protection around us as your children for we plead the blood of Jesus over our life. Help us to choose your Father and not the world. Give us deliverance of anything that is of this fallen world. We ask this in the blessed name of Jesus.

A PRAYER FOR THE SICK

JAMES CHAPTER 5 VERSE 15

Almighty God give us the faith that we need to go through the trials that come along with our sickness. I know that this will require us to the keep the faith even when we have no way of knowing what the outcome is going to be. Lord help us to keep praising you whether we feel like it or not. It is through this praise that we keep our eyes on you. When our eyes are on you we have no time to feel sorry for ourselves.

Keep us full of your presence so that you might do the work of healing in our body. When sickness comes help us to remain strong in you. These are the hard times that make us ask the question, why me? These are the times that we grow weak, uncertain, scared and confused. Please help us to remember that you love us and care about us because you are our Father in Heaven.

We live in a fallen world and we all have our crosses to bare. The way we bare our crosses is in your strength and your covering of our faith. Help us keep our eyes prayerfully on you and not look to the right or the left so we can feel your presence and receive the blessing of healing whether through mind, body and our soul.

The healing of the mine is just as beneficial to the healing of the body because the mind is the gateway to heal in power of both body and soul. Let us keep all negative energy away from your presence so that your light can shine on us. Help us to surround ourselves with the word, praises and songs of praise. In this way the protection of God is around us in out time of spiritual need and we can not be pulled down by the trappings of the world. If we are pulled down I thank you for your protection and your forgiveness.